MICHAEL HITCHCOCK

INDONESIAN
TEXTILE TECHNIQUES

SHIRE ETHNOGRAPHY

2

Cover photograph
This Biman body-tension loom was made on commission for the Pitt Rivers Museum by Idrus Yahya, Siti Samsia and Halimah M. Said. It has a discontinuous warp and is set up to weave a supplementary weft pattern with serried ranks of heddles. Mrs Diyan Leake is shown demonstrating the use of the sword in the museum. To her right are the shuttle case with spool, the sword rest and a basket containing fresh yarn.
(Copyright: Pitt Rivers Museum.)

In memory of Princess Kalisom of Bima,
whose enthusiasm for Indonesian textiles was always an inspiration.

British Library Cataloguing in Publication Data available.

Published by
SHIRE PUBLICATIONS LTD
Cromwell House, Church Street, Princes Risborough,
Aylesbury, Bucks HP17 9AJ, UK

Series Editor: Bryan Cranstone

ISBN 0 85263 769 1

First published 1985

Set in 11 point Times and printed in Great Britain by C. I. Thomas & Sons (Haverfordwest) Ltd, Press Buildings, Merlins Bridge, Haverfordwest, Dyfed.

Contents

LIST OF ILLUSTRATIONS 4
1. INTRODUCTION 5
2. TEXTILES AND SOCIETY 17
3. MATERIALS 27
4. LOOMS 36
5. DECORATIVE TECHNIQUES 45
6. MUSEUMS TO VISIT 54
7. FURTHER READING 55
INDEX 56

Acknowledgements

I generally acknowledge the contribution of Marie J. Adams, Rita Bolland, Alfred Bühler, Isaac Burkhill, Mattiebelle Gittinger and Garrett and Bronwen Solyom in this field. Permission to publish photographs of their collections was kindly granted by the Horniman Museum, Merseyside County Museums, the Museum of Mankind, Pitt Rivers Museum and the Royal Scottish Museum. In addition I should like to thank Ruth Barnes, Bernard Brandham, Bryan Cranstone, Diyan Leake, Peter Narracott and Jaqueline Palsma for their help in producing this book. My thanks are also due to the members of La Mbila and my friends in the regency of Bima and to Daina Griva, who made many suggestions regarding the text. The initial fieldwork was carried out with a grant from the Social Science Research Council and permission from Lembaga Ilmu Pendidikan Indonesia.

Where not otherwise stated, the illustrations are the author's copyright.

List of illustrations

1. Dong-son style patterns on a Sumatran cloth *page 7*
2. Sumba textile with a pattern from a Dutch coin *page 7*
3. Map of Indonesia *pages 8-9*
4. Javan batik cloth with eagle wing pattern *page 11*
5. Gold leaf on a Javan batik textile *page 13*
6. A craftswoman using a tapestry technique *page 14*
7. Javan batik cloth with shadow puppet patterns *page 16*
8. Bamboo shoot and star patterns on a Sumatran cloth *page 19*
9. Skull tree design on a Sumba textile *page 20*
10. Newlyweds receiving a textile gift *page 20*
11. Ship-of-the-dead cloth from Sumatra *page 22*
12. Timorese textile decorated with soul birds *page 23*
13. Double ikat fabric from Bali *page 24*
14. Highland farmers wearing *sarungs page 25*
15. A cotton gin *page 28*
16. Young woman pounding cotton *page 29*
17. A spindle *page 29*
18. A spinning wheel *page 29*
19. A swift *page 31*
20. Rayon fibre shoulder cloth from Bima *page 31*
21. Natural dyes on a Timorese textile *page 34*
22. Basic principles of weaving *page 36*
23. The method of leashing *page 36*
24. The weaver's cross *page 36*
25. Warping-up frame *page 37*
26. Body-tension loom with continuous warp *page 39*
27. Diagram of body-tension loom with discontinuous warp *page 40*
28. Spool and shuttle *page 40*
29. Diagram of a shaft loom *page 41*
30. Textile measurements based on the body *page 42*
31. The ikat technique *page 44*
32. Batak warp ikat textile *page 44*
33. Buginese style checked cloth *page 44*
34. Examples of tapestry weaves *page 46*
35. The supplementary weft technique *page 49*
36. A Javan batik tool *page 50*
37. Clip used in batik process *page 50*
38. The *pelangi* method *page 51*
39. Three techniques used on the same cloth *page 53*
40. Balinese painted textiles *page 53*

1
Introduction

Textiles in Indonesia

Textiles as items of aesthetic, ritual and economic significance lie at the very heart of Indonesian culture. The people of this vast archipelago make use of a wide range of techniques to produce designs of great ingenuity, and while specific styles and methods characterise the fabrics of different ethnic groups they frequently share common themes and uses. The tradition has never been static and new patterns and materials are continually being adapted to local needs and to satisfy the developing custom-made and tourist markets.

It is uncertain when textiles were first produced in Indonesia or whence they came, though carved reliefs on the walls of Borobudur, Java's ninth-century temple complex, indicate a heritage of some antiquity. Because textiles themselves are not as durable as stone and metal and do not survive to great antiquity in Indonesia's tropical climate, their history is difficult to trace. It is clear, however, that this sophisticated tradition represents the culmination of numerous generations of experience. In the centuries before the industrial manufacture of aniline dyes in Europe, Indonesia was an important source of natural dye plants, and it was Indonesian indigo, for instance, that could be produced in sufficiently large and therefore cheap quantities to supply seventeenth-century Dutch burghers with their dark cloths.

Designs which are thought to be very ancient can still be seen in modern textiles, among them the angular maze-like patterns on cloths from Sumatra and Kalimantan, which resemble the designs of the Dong-son peoples who lived on the south-east Asian mainland over two thousand years ago. Sometimes patterns from foreign textiles have been incorporated into Indonesian designs, such as those from the *patola* cloths of Gujarat in India once traded in the archipelago, or those found on Sumba which resemble the heraldic animals on old Dutch coins. Conversely, Indonesian textile designs and techniques have not remained confined to these islands: in West Africa Javan *batik* techniques have contributed to a flourishing industry, and in Europe resist-dye techniques used prior to weaving have become popular with designers and craft enthusiasts. The Indonesian word for the latter method, *ikat,* has now joined batik in the international technical vocabulary.

Geography

The Republic of Indonesia extends from the western tip of Sumatra to the centre of the island of New Guinea, a distance greater than that between London and Moscow. Although a large portion of the world's surface is enclosed within its borders, much of the territory is sea. It includes the famous islands of Java and Bali and shares the large island of Borneo with the neighbouring states of Malaysia and Brunei, the Indonesian part being known as Kalimantan.

Lying close to the equator, the islands experience a tropical climate with little variation from an average daily temperature of approximately 80 Fahrenheit (27 Celsius). Most of the islands lie in the path of monsoon winds, which bring wet weather from November to April and drier conditions for the remainder of the year, the dry season being particularly pronounced in the chain of islands to the east of Bali known as Nusa Tenggara.

The archipelago lies along an extremely active volcanic zone, which was responsible for the world's largest ever eruption, that at Tambora on Sumbawa Island in 1815. The better known but second largest eruption, that of Krakatau, took place between Java and Sumatra in 1883. Volcanic activity has thrown up high mountain ridges along the axes of the islands, while the resultant ash coupled with erosion from heavy tropical rainfall has produced fertile alluvial plains along the coasts. Lush equatorial rain forest is the natural vegetation on most of the islands, but to the east monsoon woodland and savannah are more common. In Irian Jaya, the western and Indonesian half of New Guinea, the lofty mountain peaks retain snow caps throughout the year and at the higher altitudes distinctive mountain vegetation proliferates. Kalimantan differs greatly from the other major islands because of its lack of substantial mountains. Its low-lying hills and plains are divided by numerous rivers and channels, and the extensive rain forests host a great variety of rare plants and animal species.

History

The remains of *Homo erectus* in the Solo river valley show that prehistoric hominid populations (Java man) once lived in Indonesia; it is not known, however, when the direct ancestors of the modern population first became established. Archaeological

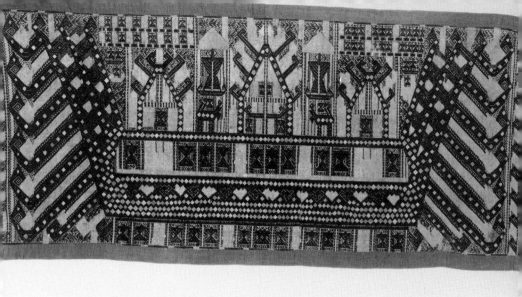

1. Geometric patterns similar to the ancient Dong-son type decorate this ceremonial cloth, *pelapai*, from Lampung in Sumatra. Cotton supplementary weft in crimson, yellow, beige and black with silver threads. 135 by 31½ inches (343 by 80 cm). (Copyright: Royal Scottish Museum.)

2. The heraldic stamp on an old Dutch coin was the inspiration for the design on this shoulder cloth, *hinggi*, from Sumba. Cotton warp ikat in russet, blue, beige and white. 50 by 23½ inches (127 by 60 cm).

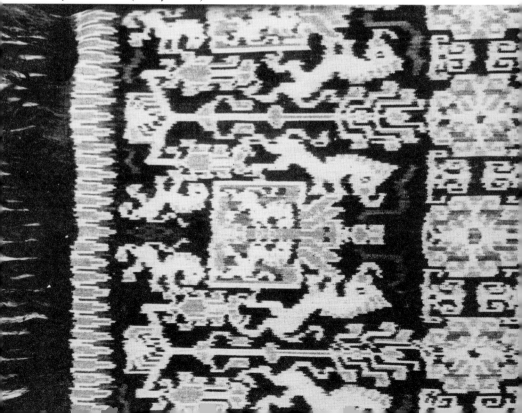

3. Map of Indonesia.

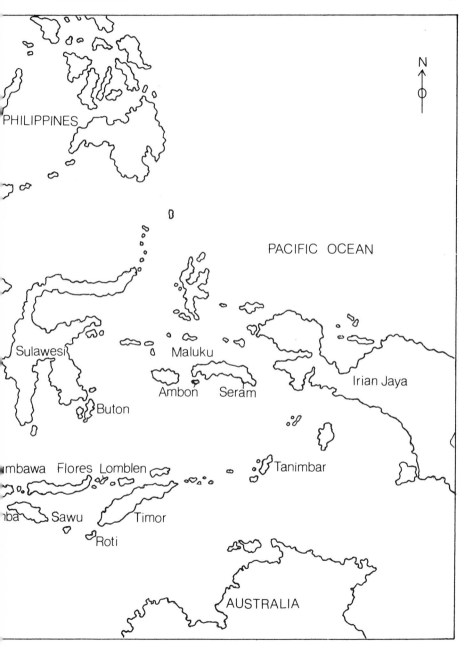

finds of weapons, pottery and gongs, and numerous standing stones are evidence of a long history.

Indigenous written accounts commence after the spread of branches of Hinduism (and later Buddhism) to the archipelago after AD100. Religious ideas and customs of Indian origin were taken by local rulers and adapted to Indonesian circumstances. Several large empires espousing Indian philosophies developed in Java and Sumatra, and on the central Javan plateau there are ruins of many fine temples. It was in this period that the world's largest Buddhist shrine and the southern hemisphere's most extensive building was constructed at Borobudur in Java. Unification of the islands was almost achieved when the great Javan-based empire of Majapahit (1294-1478) claimed suzerainty over a territory approaching the size of modern Indonesia.

Hindu power declined when Islam, which had been brought by southern Arabian and Muslim Indian traders, spread inland from the coast and with the demise of Majapahit in the fifteenth century many court officials and priests fled to the safety of Bali to the east. Today most Indonesians profess Islam, but the island of Bali steadfastly retains its Buddhist/Hindu traditions.

Shortly after this the Portuguese ventured across the Indian Ocean in search of spices. With Islam firmly planted in the western islands, Portuguese and later Dutch proselytising was largely restricted to the east, and now Christian communities are found throughout eastern Nusa Tenggara, central Sulawesi (Celebes) and Maluku (the Moluccas). Although the Portuguese attained an early command over the archipelago's trade, they were ousted by the Dutch in the seventeenth century; nevertheless, they maintained a colonial presence in the region longer than any other foreign power and withdrew from East Timor only in 1974. They have had a marked impact on Indonesian culture, Portuguese influences being apparent in both music and the decorative arts, particularly in the east.

Based in its purpose-built headquarters at Batavia (later called Jakarta, the modern republic's capital), the Dutch East India Company became the dominant mercantile power. At first Dutch goals were limited to trade, especially the extremely profitable clove business of Maluku, but the extension of their business interests gradually embroiled them in local politics. The company's success was not long-lasting and by the eighteenth century its imminent collapse on the Amsterdam stock exchange prompted the Dutch government to take control of its assets, and especially its Indonesian possessions — the Netherlands' colonial

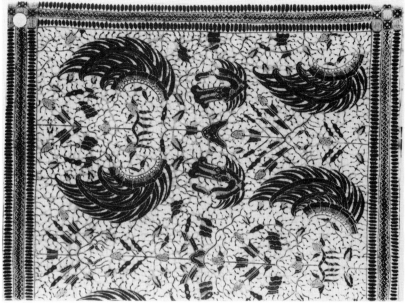

4. These eagle-wing patterns show evidence of Java's Hindu history, taken from representations of Garuda, the mythological mount of Vishnu. Cotton batik in cream, russet and umber. 101 by 20 inches (257 by 51 cm). (Copyright: Horniman Museum.)

empire was born.

Except for a brief period of British control during the Napoleonic Wars, the Dutch remained the foremost power in Indonesia until the twentieth century. Their rule was a common colonial medley of harsh exploitation in one hand and the development of numerous technical benefits on the other. Commodities, such as rubber, which are still economically significant were introduced and Dutch international connections provided a boost for the Indonesian dyes trade. Colonisation was not without its bloody campaigns, but ironically it was Dutch education and European political ideals which helped to expose the contradictions of the colonial system, and by the end of their rule nationalism had become an important political force.

In 1942 Dutch imperial pretensions collapsed in the face of the Japanese advance. These new conquerors needed local support for their over-extended war effort and some nationalist groups were provided with military training, later to prove useful for their own purposes. Most Indonesians welcomed the collapse of the harsh Japanese interregnum in 1945 and the nationalists, fearing further colonial rule, proclaimed the Indonesian Republic. The only remaining Dutch possession, Irian Jaya, was ceded to the republic by a United Nations mandate in 1969. Indonesia's boundaries were extended yet again when it annexed the newly independent territory of East Timor, despite protests from the Portuguese government.

The people

During the twentieth century there has been a massive expansion in Indonesia's population and now it is the world's fifth most populous state. Most of the people are, however, concentrated on the extremely fertile islands of Java, Madura and Bali. In contrast, Sumatra, Kalimantan and Irian Jaya are sparsely populated and in recent years the government has tried to ease overcrowding on the land by encouraging farmers to resettle.

Most people have light brown complexions, dark straight hair and dark eyes. They speak many languages and dialects, which are an important means of differentiating between ethnic groups: on Java, for instance, the inhabitants of the centre and east speak Javanese while in the west they use Sundanese. Most of the languages belong to the Austronesian family in the same way that English belongs to the Indo-European language group (Austronesian is a very extended family, with its speakers being found in five south-east Asian states and such far-flung places as Madagascar and parts of Oceania). In the modern Indonesian Republic these diverse peoples are united by a common language, similar to Malay, which was spread by traders to the numerous ports. Indonesian gained currency as a *lingua franca* when it became an official Dutch medium of communication and today it is the national language.

In Irian Jaya and some of its nearby islands most of the population differ from other Indonesians by their Melanesian appearance and their use of non-Austronesian languages. Their striking craft industries do not belong to the heritage of Indonesian textiles and will not be discussed here.

Indonesian societies

Along the coastlines of Indonesia can be found communities of traders and fishermen who may be ethnically different from the inland dwellers and who share a common culture with other sea peoples. Two groups, the Bajo Laut, who originally came from the Sulu Sea, and the Buginese, who have spread throughout the islands from their homeland in southern Sulawesi, retain aspects

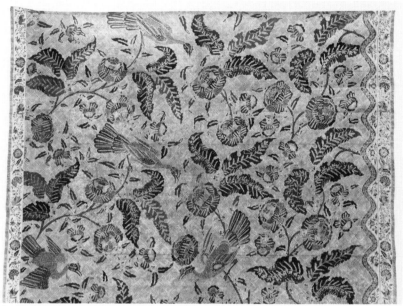

5. Gold leaf secured by paste adorns this prestige fabric from Java. Cotton batik in red, green, cream, blue and purple. 81½ by 42 inches (205 by 107 cm). (Copyright: Royal Scottish Museum.)

of their original languages. In general these people are more involved in commerce than government and are often noted for staunch Muslim traditions.

On the islands themselves the climate frequently permits the cultivation of up to three crops a year by intensive irrigation schemes. Large food surpluses could be produced with the Indonesian wet rice, paddy, and these were used to support elaborate bureaucratic systems, especially in Java. Today the majority of the population still resides in villages in the wet rice farming regions, though the old royal capitals support national administrations. Developing industries exist in some of the cities, many of which have been swollen by rural migration.

Further inland, in the forests and highlands, many people use swidden techniques to farm plots of land for short periods, virgin land being opened periodically and exhausted fields being left fallow. In contrast to the lowland or coastal people, these small-scale interior-living societies often emphasise distinctive systems of knowledge and belief and may not be so deeply immersed in the world religions.

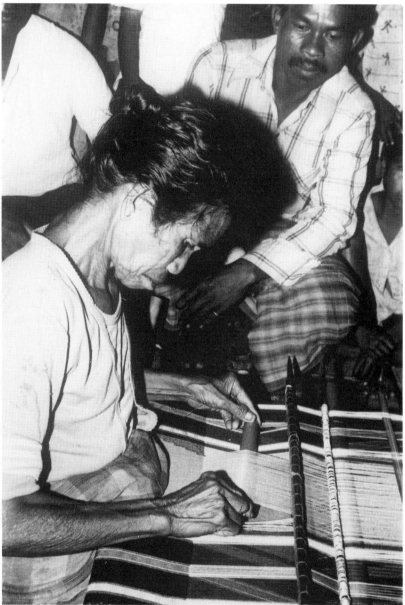

6. A Biman craftswoman from Ntobo is braced in a body-tension loom and using a tapestry technique to make a shoulder cloth, *seledang*.

Craft workers

The archipelago is particularly well known for its work in precious and base metals, carpentry, basketry, weaving and dyeing. Before the formation of the republic the best craft workers were often encouraged under royal patronage to settle near the palaces of the many kingdoms. Skilled craft work boosted the prestige of sultans and princes; while royal families are no longer politically powerful many continue to take an interest in these arts (especially in Jogyakarta and Surakarta in Java).

In the past crafts were practised at all social levels and some of the finest weavers were of the most noble lineages. Craft skills are found in most villages although there does tend to be some specialisation as certain areas become famous for making particular products. It is quite common to find most craftswomen in one village making baskets and then find that the majority of the next are weavers. In some parts of Indonesia there may be whole regions where people do not produce cloth and therefore have to obtain it by trade from their neighbours.

The young republic is trying to industrialise rapidly and some crafts have declined through the loss of skilled people to new industries and through local or foreign factory competition for craft products. Some domestic industries have survived and indeed flourished by exploiting the regional and custom-made markets that are not so easily penetrated by factory-based competition. Because textiles are important symbols of regional identity in a multi-ethnic state, the small industries often have a constant local demand. Furthermore, the flexible domestic producer is well adapted to the custom-made market, where contact between manufacturer and consumer is required, and this may be particularly the case when ritual textiles are being designed. Prestige crafts have often continued around the old royal centres by catering for modern administrators, and tourists have been keen, if not always aesthetically attuned, buyers of local products.

The manufacturer may be the person who sells the goods in one of Indonesia's numerous markets, but more often it is a small-scale local trader who is known to the craftswoman and may be a relative. Goods may also be peddled from door to door and it is not uncommon to see saleswomen laden with textiles walking between villages. Fixed prices are seldom attached to the goods and bargaining is customary, this usually being a relaxed but swift affair since most local people have a shrewd idea of the approximate value of these products.

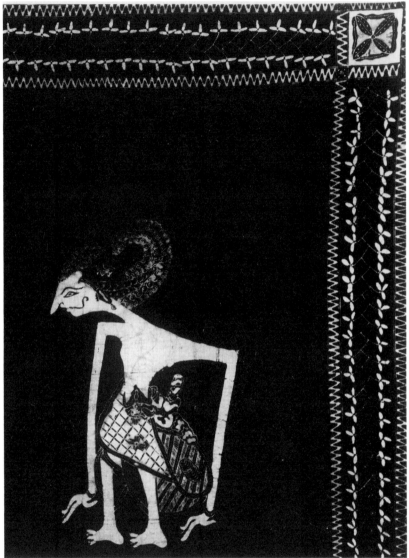

7. Characters from the Javan shadow theatre decorate this *kain* that was probably made for the tourist market. Cotton batik *tulis* in blue and cream. 101 by 42 inches (257 by 107 cm). (Copyright: Horniman Museum.)

2
Textiles and society

Women and textiles

Anthropological research in Indonesia has revealed a fairly consistent sexual division of labour with regard to crafts, usually without any hierarchical connotations: men's and women's crafts are complementary rather then competitive. The most common division is that of metalworking by men and the production of textiles by women. Men also tend to undertake such tasks as boat and house building while women practise basketry and pottery, although it is only in the Muslim areas where men usually perform the heavier tasks. All the jobs associated with manufacturing textiles, such as harvesting cotton, dyeing and weaving, are controlled by women and income earned from these activities belongs to them. Men, however, may be involved in aspects of textile design and usually make equipment such as looms and spinning wheels.

Although textile schools have been set up to encourage regional traditions, the majority of weavers learn through practical experience by imitating their senior female relatives. A young girl of five or six may begin by learning basic tasks in the company of her mother, gradually acquiring new skills in an informal education. By her early teens she is expected to be competent in the regional skills of patterning textiles, although the greatest experts are usually older women.

Given the complementary character of men's and women's tasks, a good craftswoman is considered a desirable marriage partner and in the past young women were sometimes expected to advertise their skills to potential husbands. In especially pious Muslim communities girls could not work in full public view and they broadcast their industriousness by attaching noise-makers to their looms which rattled as they worked. Amongst the Bimanese of Sumbawa island there are tales of suitors reciting love quatrains beneath the windows where young women worked, the success of their suit being gauged by the level of rattling emitting from the loom. A model of a Bugis loom in Cambridge with a clapper built into the warp-beam may indicate similar romantic associations.

Designs and colours

In pre-republican days the highest members of society,

especially the courtiers, monopolised the most attractive designs and most expensive materials. The patterns were recorded on lattices of palm leaf and bamboo, and a successful weaver or dyer usually also had access to a stock of old textiles to which she could refer. Today, while the knowledge of designs is more widespread, it is generally the older weavers who record successful creations for future reference, often aided by photographs and graph paper.

The design of a new textile is quite eclectic, sometimes involving long discussions between the craftswoman and the customer. Although traditional guidelines concerning the selection of pattern and colour may be followed, innovation, either by rearrangement of existing designs or by the addition of new elements, is also appreciated. Even personal touches, such as the name of the customer, may be included. It is perhaps this willingness to be varied that has facilitated the introduction of new ideas from neighbouring and foreign sources. The bamboo shoot, *tumpal*, and the eight-pointed star or mangosteen designs are found on many islands and appear to be ancient patterns. In contrast, the *patola* patterns that are used in many Indonesian textiles are clearly traceable to cloth from Gujarat in India which was traded throughout the archipelago in the nineteenth century.

The aesthetics of colour are important and different societies possess their own guidelines concerning the combination and selection of hues. In central Java, for instance, blue, brown, cream and green are thought to be the most refined colours, and although this region's two great capitals employ all of them and have many intricate designs in common, the large blocks of colour in the form of central lozenges and rectangles belong to Surakarta's repertoire. Generally, the colours of Java are restrained, and these contrast markedly with the bright hues preferred in the west of Nusa Tenggara and in southern Sulawesi.

Before the formation of the republic many Indonesian societies had class systems with a royal family at the top. Beneath them was a class we might regard as an aristocracy while the majority of people would have been commoners. Some societies had a middle class between the commoners and nobles, and there were sometimes slaves. A person's rank and occupation could be indicated by the textiles he wore and they were therefore potent status symbols. On Sumba the upper classes tried to restrict the manufacture and ownership of complex ikat fabrics and M. J. Adams tells us that they may have been able to punish violations of dress rules until the 1920s and 1930s. Colour was significant in

8. Pan-Indonesian bamboo shoot and eight-pointed star designs can be seen on this fabric from Palembang in Sumatra. Silk weft ikat centre panel in crimson, orange, violet and green with borders in a gilded supplementary weft. 102 by 43 inches (259 by 109 cm). (Copyright: Royal Scottish Museum.)

some societies such as the Bimanese, where troops wore red as an indication of their bravery and civil servants had black and blue checked clothing to symbolise their loyalty. The materials used could also be communicative, particularly gold, which is widely associated with political success: on Nias a leader used to wear a gold-embellished costume at the ceremony that promoted him to a higher rank.

Indonesia's textile designs are a good indicator of the values of its people. Family relationships and friends, for example, are important to many islanders and these are illustrated in textiles made by Sumatran Bataks which show rows of people holding hands. For the wet-rice farmer the water buffalo is an indispensable draught animal and buffalo designs appear on the cloths of the Toraja of central Sulawesi and the Timorese. The skull imagery of Sumba harks back to the days when heads were taken in warfare and displayed on trees outside the victorious households, although the modern use of these designs is more for aesthetic then bellicose reasons.

Social and ritual use

Textiles are valuable items of trade and are often stored in a trunk in a secure part of the house. They are especially important for the mobile seafaring and swidden-cultivating communities

9. *(above)* Skull tree motifs recall warfare in Sumba's history. Cotton supplementary warp in red, yellow, white and black. 86 by 26 inches (128 by 66 cm). (Copyright: Museum of Mankind.)

10. *(left)* Dressed as nobles, these Biman newly-weds receive a gift of a textile.

because they are easily stored and portable and can be quickly converted into cash or exchanged for other commmodities in times of emergency. As has been mentioned, the manufacture of textiles is an important source of income for many craftswomen. The economic value of textiles was once taken to its logical outcome in Buton in the sixteenth-century when special fabrics were used as currency; indeed the financial value of cloth is an aspect of their ceremonial significance, as was the case in Lampung on Sumatra, where elaborate textiles, known as *pelapai*, were displayed on the walls by the person hosting an important social gathering.

In common with many south-east Asian societies, Indonesians hold festivals to mark each stage of a person's transition through life. On these occasions special food such as glutinous rice or cakes may be eaten, with perhaps a reading from the Koran (in the case of Muslims), and ritual textiles are often displayed or exchanged. In Biman society textiles appear at the earliest possible moment when babies are laid on a white cloth that symbolises goodness and purity. Fabrics more commonly appear at festivals held later in childhood and Sven Cedroth describes them being washed and then stored in the sacred pavilion in north Lombok where the boys' transitional hair-cutting ritual is performed.

One of the most important uses of textiles is as ritual gifts which are given as women's goods from the bride's family to the bridegroom's in exchange for men's goods. These exchanges usually take place at festivals held before the wedding and the marriage can only take place when all the requirements have been satisfied. Sometimes, as was the case amongst the Sundanese, a young woman had to weave a special fabric before she could get married, though this is no longer very common. Even though marriages are usually arranged between families, this procedure occasionally breaks down and the young couple elope together without the usual gift exchanges. Such failures in negotiation have different causes ranging from the inability of one family to comply with the required exchange of gifts to the urgencies of romantic love. One solution to the problem of unfulfilled gift exchanges has been recorded by Mattiebelle Gittinger in Lampung, where the normal procedure is reversed: it is the young man who provides the textile by leaving a special 'elopement' cloth on the floor of the girl's room. This gift helps to ease the couple's reintegration into society at a later date. In normal circumstances textiles are conspicuously displayed at wedding celebrations when friends and relatives come to congratulate the bridal couple. On these occasions the newly-weds don regional costumes, sometimes similar to those once worn by royalty, and receive the guests while standing on a raised podium: behind them precious heirloom textiles are frequently hung.

Funerals are another occasion when textiles make an appearance. Robert Barnes recorded the observation of a specific etiquette in Kédang on Lomblen, where relatives of the deceased bring pieces of cloth to the graveside, the colour of the fabric indicating their relationship by marriage. Aspects of a legendary

11. An elephant and people travel on a 'ship-of-the-dead' across a sea rich in fishes and sky replete with birds and mythical creatures. *Tampan* from Lampung in Sumatra. Cotton supplementary weft in crimson, blue and beige. 29½ by 27½ inches (75 by 70 cm). (Copyright: Royal Scottish Museum.)

12. Soul birds, their stomachs filled with rice, and ancestor figures decorate this man's shoulder blanket, *selimut,* from Timor. Cotton warp ikat with fringes, indigo blue and undyed centre panel; pink, yellow and black borders. 80 by 46½ inches (204 by 118 cm).

afterlife may also appear on textiles, and those in Lampung and the Semawan part of Sumbawa used to be embellished with 'ships-of-the-dead' containing the souls of the deceased with all the possessions they would need in their future existence. Similarly Timorese textiles are sometimes decorated with birds, which are associated with souls.

Apart from the life cycle festivals, textiles have other ceremonial uses. In Bali, for example, long cloths called *lamak* are hung in temples on specific holy days and textiles are often used when houses are being erected, and in many eastern islands fabrics that are attached to house posts are likened to sails, maritime imagery being often associated with houses amongst people whose livelihoods are closely connected with the sea. Textiles generally

13. Several years are sometimes needed to make these 'lucky' *gerinsing* textiles from Tenganan in Bali. Cotton double ikat in umber, russet and beige. 83 by 19½ inches (211 by 49 cm). (Copyright: Pitt Rivers Museum.)

have positive mystical associations throughout Indonesia and this is particularly so with the complicated double ikats of Bali, *gerinsing,* which are thought to be able to ward off evil. Similar protective qualities are ascribed to textiles on many islands, the culturally important wavy-bladed daggers called *kris* being wrapped in them when not in use.

Weavers and dyers who are engaged in manufacturing these ritually important textiles often prepare themselves by fasting and meditating before commencing work. For the Balinese makers of the double ikats these preparations would be extensive and in Pekalongan in Java women stay awake through the night burning incense before the work starts. This contrasts with Bimanese weavers, who, in similar circumstances, simply prepare a small ritual meal.

Clothing

Textiles can be used to make many types of clothing, the most common being: the *kain,* a cloth that is wrapped around the hips; the *sarung,* a similar textile sewn into a tube; the *selimut,* a

14. Homespun and factory-made *sarungs* combine with modern shirts and trousers in the clothing of these highland farmers from the Wawo language area of Bima.

shoulder cloth or blanket; the *selendang*, a scarf, shawl or sash; and the *destar*, a cloth worn on the head.

The *kain* is popular in Java, Madura, Bali and western Lombok and is worn by both sexes. It is usually tied around the waist by wrapping around the front and back and by tucking in the loose end near the left hip. An attractive pleat may be allowed to hang in front of the wearer and in Java women sometimes starch it into numerous neat folds. Apart from being a garment, the *kain* can be used for numerous other purposes such as bedspread or table cloth and be secured in different ways to make bundles for market produce.

On Indonesia's other islands it is the *sarung* that is most commonly worn. The wearer usually steps into the tube, pulling the sides up around the body. Men tie it into a fold in front of the navel, whereas women often gather and tuck it in on the left hip. The *sarung* can also be worn by tucking it under the armpits or by tying it over the shoulder in a knot. In east Flores these garments could be secured on the shoulders with thorns and in Bima they are sometimes worn over the head like a veil. Like the ubiquitous

kain, the *sarung* can have many uses: it is popular as nightwear
and for carrying merchandise; it can serve as a baby's cradle while
the parents work in the field and may provide protection from
chilly sea breezes on the decks of ships at night. Seamen often
wear a *sarung* over a pair of shorts so that during work it can be
tucked around the waist to keep the legs free and upon returning
home or going to attend business the cloth can be let down to
provide a more formal garment. Indonesian businessmen and
civil servants often wear a lightweight suit to work and yet prefer
a *sarung* or *kain* for relaxing at home in the evening. For festivals
the traditional garments are nearly always worn.

The *selimut* reaches its most spectacular form on the islands of
eastern Nusa Tenggara. Because it was once worn as a sign of
rank it is usually elaborately decorated and has fringes at either
end. The *selimut* is usually worn over the shoulder and is either
tied on the opposite hip or secured with a belt as is common in
Roti, Sawu and Timor.

The *selendang* may range from the size of a small *selimut* to a
narrow band and it is in the latter form that it is worn over the
shoulder in the Indonesian national costume. Sometimes the
selendang doubles up as a kind of shawl and can frequently be
seen worn around the waist as a colourful sash.

Head cloths, *destar*, are often no bigger than about 4 square
feet (0.37 sq m) and may be reduced to a simple triangle of
material. The manner of tying the cloth varies from island to
island: for instance, in central Java the cloth can be pulled tight
around the forehead and tied at the nape of the neck, whereas in
neighbouring Madura it is folded into a triangle and tied so that a
flap projects upwards at the back. This flap may be tucked
forwards, as is the case in Bali, or moved around to the front and
allowed to stick upwards, as in southern Sulawesi. Numerous
variations, sometimes requiring complicated methods of folding,
are found throughout the archipelago.

Other popular garments include the long Javan cloths, *stagen*,
that are wrapped repeatedly around the stomach and the long
narrow loincloths, *cawat*, of the various peoples of inner
Kalimantan.

3
Materials

Yarns

Cotton may not be native to south-east Asia, but it has always been the predominant textile material. Our earliest knowledge of it in the archipelago comes from Palembang in Sumatra, where Chinese merchants purchased cotton fabrics in the seventh century. When the Portuguese arrived they found domestic cotton industries already well established and production began to decline only in the nineteenth century when the world market was flooded by plantation-grown and factory-processed goods from the north Atlantic seaboard. Dutch attempts to protect the local industry temporarily succeeded in parts of Sumatra and Java and in islands such as Sulawesi the production of specialist cottons (for example, calico) ensured the industry's survival. Small-scale manufacturing also persisted in eastern Indonesia, with Timor being one of the foremost producers. During the Second World War the Japanese, urgently requiring cloth, attempted to stimulate the industry by introducing new strains, but their efforts were largely unsuccessful. Despite unfavourable fluctuations in world markets, cotton production has continued in the eastern islands, where domestic means of spinning can still be seen.

One of the commonest strains in eastern Indonesia is *Gossypium herbaceum,* a cotton of Old World origin. Although it can be easily spun, its fibres contain a fuzz that can make it difficult to weave. It is the fuzz which gives many east Indonesian textiles their characteristic thickness, a trait that is much appreciated in cooler, highland areas. At the height of the industry in Java cotton was often grown as a second crop in the paddy fields during the dry season. In the eastern islands today it may be cultivated on hillside swiddens or gathered from abandoned fields where it grows wild.

Although some methods of preparing cotton for weaving are found throughout Indonesia, others may exhibit regional variation. The first stage is ginning. The cotton gin shown in fig. 15 is similar to those found on most islands: it consists of an upright frame supporting two rollers, which are turned by a handle to press out the seeds from the raw cotton. Wooden wedges can be added to alter the pressure between the rollers and the whole apparatus is held firm by a wooden base, which often has a

15. An Indonesian cotton gin collected by the author. (Copyright: Pitt Rivers Museum.)

projecting foot to aid stability.

On some islands, such as Java and Sumbawa, spinners further untangle the cotton by the use of a bow or cotton beaters. In the first method, which is preferred by older women, the string of a bamboo bow is strummed across the fibres to fluff them up into a neat pile. Younger women prefer the second method, which entails thumping the cotton with two rattan beaters on a hide mat. Rhythms set up by the beating are sometimes accompanied by songs.

Cotton fibres are formed for spinning into convenient hand-sized cylinders by rolling a spindle across the cotton on a flat stone. Spinning wheels are used on all the major islands as far east as Sulawesi, but further east the spindle alone is used. In the former method a wheel, turned by a handle, drives a spindle by means of a belt. Sitting on the floor with the apparatus to her right, the spinner attaches fresh fibres to the spindle and as she rotates the wheel she draws the cotton cylinder away to form a yarn. Where the spinning wheel is not used, the spindle, weighted with a spindle whorl, is turned by hand and then allowed to drop so that it spins the yarn as it falls. In both techniques the freshly spun thread is wound on to the spindle after each draw.

16. *(above left)* A young Biman woman pounds cotton on a goatskin with rattan beaters. She wears *sarungs* around both her hips and shoulders.

17. *(above right)* A spindle weighted with a wooden spindle whorl of the type used in East Nusa Tenggara.

18. *(below)* An Indonesian spinning wheel collected by the author. (Copyright: Pitt Rivers Museum.)

The spun yarn is usually unwound from the spindle and looped around an H-shaped frame to form skeins. These skeins can then easily be placed on a swift, the freely rotating arms of which enable the weaver to draw off thread smoothly as it is required. An arrangement of the spinning wheel and swift may be used to wind thread on to a cylindrical spool. This is achieved by attaching the thread to a spool placed on the spindle tip, so that when the wheel is turned thread is drawn off the swift.

Silk is the most valued yarn although its history in the archipelago is uncertain. Neither the moths whose cocoons are used for silk filaments nor the mulberry trees, on which they feed, are indigenous. Both come from China and yet despite that nation's long trade links with the islands the Indonesian word for silk, *sutra,* is of Indian origin. Although silk goods may have been traded by the Chinese, perhaps the knowledge of its manufacture was introduced via India. Despite the successful cultivation of mulberries in parts of Java and Maluku, most of Indonesia's modern needs are fulfilled by the silk industries of Ujung Pandang in Sulawesi.

Several species of moth yield the gluey substances that can be drawn into silk filaments, though the most popular for commercial purposes is *Bombyx mori.* The filaments have to be extracted before complete metamorphosis because the emerging moth usually excretes a fluid that weakens the cocoon fibres. Hot moist air is therefore used to stifle the pupa, after which the cocoons are unwound in hot water, which helps to dissolve the material, sterecine, that binds the coils together. But because a single filament is not strong enough to weave alone, four or five of them are glued together with some of the binding material that has been retained.

Synthetic thread (mainly rayon) is widely available in Indonesia and has been adapted to the handloom industry, particularly in the eastern islands, Sumatra and north Bali. It come from a number of sources, notably Java and Hong Kong, and is popular as it is lightweight and easy to weave because the threads do not break as easily as cotton. Furthermore, the colours are more varied than those readily available by local means and they do not fade as quickly as most vegetable dyes.

Metallic threads, especially gold and silver, are popular in most of Sumatra, coastal Kalimantan, Bali and Sumbawa. Although some precious metals are mined in Indonesia, they are usually imported; in the colonial period they were brought in, in the form of Dutch coins, which were melted down by village craftsmen.

Materials

19. *(right)* An Indonesian swift, with compartments in the base for a betel-chewing kit, collected by the author. (Copyright: Pitt Rivers Museum.)

20. *(below)* Modern fibres, rayon, were woven by hand to make this typical Biman shoulder cloth, *salampé*. Yellow tapestry weave centre field with black borders and many-coloured float weave stripes. 70 by 23 inches (178 by 58 cm). (Copyright: Pitt Rivers Museum.)

Gold or silver thread is often made by drawing the metal through a perforated plate (draw plate) to form a wire, which is later annealed to toughen it. The wire is then hammered into a fine ribbon and spun round a cotton or silk core. Sometimes this thread would be prepared by rolling it by hand on the thigh. As precious metal threads age they slowly come apart, allowing the core to become visible beneath the ribbon. Very often silver ribbon is not wound into a thread but is couched directly on the surface of the cloth. Gilded silver is popular for partly aesthetic and partly economic reasons.

Dyes

The process of dyeing yarn is seldom straightforward, some dyes taking better to certain fibres than others. Although there are some dyes that can be used directly, others require an auxiliary agent, known as a mordant, to fix them. With silk fibres it may also be necessary to prevent a film developing on top of the dye bath, which Indonesians sometimes achieve by including essential oils from local products such as cloves and nutmegs.

Indigo is an ancient dye and tests have revealed its use in Egyptian mummy cloths from around 2300 BC. It is impossible to determine when indigo was first used in Indonesia and it has been suggested that the ancient Chinese brought the knowledge of the dye to the archipelago. It was indigo, along with rare oriental spices and fragrant timbers, that first drew Portuguese and later other European traders to Indonesia. The Dutch East India Company increased the production of this important plant and along with the British in India they dominated the European market. Indonesian exports of indigo rose until Holland was invaded by the French in the Napoleonic Wars. Unlike the Netherlands, Britain was not occupied and it quickly filled the gap left by the Dutch and took control of this essential international commodity. From then until the close of the nineteenth century indigo production was mainly based in the British colonial possessions.

Until the chemical structure of indigo was discovered by A. von Baeyer, it was made exclusively from plant sources. Later, when the Germans began to manufacture the synthetic dye at competitive prices, the plant source of indigo ceased to be of international importance. Although the Germans had broken the British monopoly, the advent of the First World War saw a brief rise in indigo production in Java and today the plant remains a small but significant part of the Indonesian dyestuffs trade, especially in Nusa Tenggara.

Indigo is a blue powder made from plants of the genus *Indigofera,* which are grown throughout the archipelago. Farmers often used to cultivate the plants as an extra crop, and today the bushes are more usually seen growing wild around the edges of fields or along roadsides. The process by which the dye is obtained is akin to fermentation. Firstly, the leaves are pounded in a mortar and then placed in a large earthenware pot and mixed with water. The mixture is left for about a week and stirred occasionally, releasing a distinctive smell. After the impurities have been skimmed off, the thread is transferred to the pot and kneaded in the liquid. During the day the yarn is dried in sunlight and returned to the pot at night. This mild oxidation helps to convert the colourless liquid into indigo and after approximately three days the thread turns light blue. Repeated dippings are, however, needed to obtain a deeper colour, though much of this tends to run because mordants are seldom used. Alfred Bühler has noted that on Roti bark continuing tannic acid may be added in order to obtain a darker hue.

Safflower has a long history as a source of dye and was known to the ancient civilisations of Asia and North Africa. It may have spread to Indonesia from India and by the early nineteenth century had become well established in Bali, Sulawesi and Sumbawa. These islands still produce safflower, which is mainly shipped to Java.

The petals of safflower, *Carthatmus tinctorius,* yield two dyes, safflower yellow and carthamine. The petals are usually crushed, kneaded and stirred in cold water, and after they have settled the yellow liquid is poured off. The process is repeated until all the yellow colour has been separated, whereupon a small quantity of valuable red dye can be finally extracted from the petals. Unfortunately the red hue is mildly acidic and has to be rendered harmless in an alkaline solution before it can be used to dye cloth. Lime, which is easily obtained from either limestone or coral, is usually mixed with the dye to neutralise the acid. This process is widely used throughout Indonesia, though both colours are not particularly stable and tend to fade with age.

Cudrania javanensis is a spiny shrub with a heartwood that can yield a yellow dye. Much of this timber used to be exported from eastern Indonesia, especially Timor, and was extensively used in the Javan batik industry. The dye can be extracted by soaking chips of the heartwood in water for a night followed by boiling.

21. Museum storage free of ultraviolet light has perfectly preserved the intensity of the natural dyes in this early twentieth-century shoulder blanket from East (formerly Portuguese) Timor. Supplementary warp and embroidery in indigo blue, possibly morinda red and undyed cotton. 80 by 38 inches (203 by 97 cm). (Copyright: Pitt Rivers Museum.)

The water is then strained and a mordant is added. The fabric to be coloured is usually boiled in the mixture to produce yellow; however, if it is first kneaded in indigo before dyeing in *Cudrania*, then a green hue can be obtained.

Morinda is the source of a red, purple or chocolate dye that can be released from its root bark by boiling in a dilute acid. It has been popular in the Javan batik industry and amongst many of eastern Indonesia's Muslim communities. Bühler noted that the Muslims treated the thread with vegetable oils before dyeing in *Morinda*, whereas the Bataks used an animal fat preparation. In eastern Indonesia mordants made from pounded alumina-bearing plants were used with the dye, although it might take several years to produce a rich colour.

Turmeric, which belongs to the genus *Curcuma*, has long been important and may have come to Indonesia through trade with the Asian mainland. In Kalimantan the rhizomes were used for their yellow hue in preparation for dyeing red, while the Bimanese mix them with lime to achieve the same effect. Turmeric appears to have been used to produce yellow alone, usually by several immersions in the dye.

Teak trees of the genus *Tectona* grow well on the drier islands to the east and are renowned for their numerous applications in carpentry. It is less well known, however, that the leaves can sometimes be used to make a brown or red stain — a skill known in both Sumbawa and Sulawesi.

Clitorea belongs to a diverse group of plants that are lumped together as *turi* by many Indonesians. The flowers have been used in the Riau archipelago to leave a fleeting colour on white cloth.

Sesbania fruits are also called *turi* and they yield a yellow juice that is useful for colouring matting and which was occasionally used for dyeing cloth by the Bimanese.

Sappan wood, *Caesalpinia,* used to be an important source of tannin on most islands. The heartwood, which turns red on contact with air, was also a source of a fleeting russet dye, often combined with alum as a mordant.

Rhizophora mucronata, a swamp-growing tree that can yield a dye from its bark and leaves, is popular amongst the many coastal communities.

Soot from lamp-black and resin is known to produce a deep black dye on cotton cloth in Kalimantan and Tanimbar. In Sulawesi and Timor fabrics would first be dyed with indigo, the soot being painted on later.

4
Looms

Basic principles

Textiles are made by interlacing one group of threads, the weft, at right angles to another set known as the warp, and the process is called weaving. In Indonesia weaving is accomplished by means of various looms, the basic principles of which are as follows.

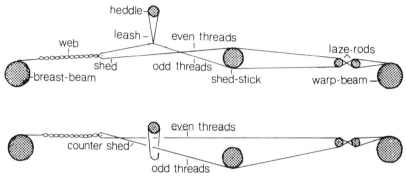

22. Basic principles of weaving (after Ling Roth).

The warp threads are stretched in parallel lines between a beam which is closest to the weaver, the breast-beam, and another that is opposite her, the warp-beam. The weaver proceeds by raising the alternate warp threads with leashes to form a space called the shed. Through this space the weft thread is placed and firmly beaten into the already woven cloth, the web, with a sword. To make the work easier the leashes are attached to a rod called the heddle so that all of them can be raised at once. When the upward pull on the heddle is released the weight of the bar, known as the shed-stick, carries the odd threads below the

23. The method of leashing.   **24.** The weaver's cross.

25. An Indonesian warping-up frame collected by the author. (Copyright: Pitt Rivers Museum.)

even ones to form a counter-shed through which the weft is entered as before. This crossing action keeps the weft in place by interlacing it between the odd and even warp threads. The distinction between the odd and even threads is further aided by laze-rods, which form a weaver's cross and thereby help to keep the warp in parallel lines.

Warping up

The threads can be more easily handled when they have been coated in a gum-like fluid known as size. This is often achieved by soaking the thread in a solution of glutinous rice or other material that will stiffen and strengthen the yarn.

Before weaving can commence the thread has to be entered into a loom by a process called warping up. The amount of warp required is longer than the finished cloth because the process of weaving causes the warp to undulate in a vertical plane as it intermeshes with the weft, thereby foreshortening its horizontal length. Therefore a considerable amount of space is required for warping up and it is usually undertaken by stretching the warp between poles that will later be replaced by the warp-beam and breast-beam. These poles can be attached to convenient trees or house posts and the weaver walks back and forth between them, letting out the thread from a spool in her hand.

Sometimes an apparatus known as a warping-up frame is used to reduce the amount of effort. The frame has two blocks of three or more upright posts and the ones that are diagonally opposite each other can be used to simulate the warp-beam and breast-beam. The thread can be zig-zagged between the poles to extend the warp fully without taking up too much space. A movable rod sometimes joins the two blocks so that the distance between them can be altered, and a weaver's cross can be formed by passing alternate warp threads on either side of a spike set into one side of the frame.

Body-tension looms

Body-tension looms are found throughout Indonesia, with the exception of inland Irian Jaya, and are so named because the pressure of the body is used to keep the warp threads in tension, a prerequisite for successful weaving.

One of the commonest types of body-tension loom is known in inner Kalimantan, Sulawesi, Bali and Nusa Tenggara. In this kind the tension is maintained by fixing the warp-beam to a convenient tree or house post, while the weaver secures the breast-beam by means of a strap which passes around her lower back. She usually sits on the ground with her feet outstretched and the warp inclined at a slight upward angle in front of her.

In order to enlarge each shed sufficiently to allow the weft to pass through, the sword is slipped in and turned on its side. When the weft is in place, the weaver leans back and beats it in (the sword is removed to change the sheds). In this kind of loom the warp threads are continuous, that is, they pass under the breast-beam and join up with those at the warp-beam to form a complete circle. As the weaver works, she keeps the sheds at a comfortable distance by pulling the finished cloth towards her and under the breast-beam. By this method the web continues to pass alongside the underside of the unwoven warp until it eventually meets the recently woven cloth. Should the cloth be required flat, then the warp has to be cut along the unwoven section. On many of these looms the breast-beam is split down the centre and the web secured between the two halves. This arrangement can be loosened to pull new cloth under the beam.

The weft is usually entered with a spool in which the yarn is wrapped lengthways parallel to its central axis. An even width of cloth can be maintained by sticking the sharp ends of a lath, called a temple, into the edges, selvages, on the underside of the fabric.

In another widely used body-tension loom the warp-beam is not attached to a post but is slotted into a heavy frame. These looms are used throughout western Indonesia, coastal Kalimantan, southern Sulawesi and as far east as Bima. The frame for holding the warp-beam often has tall wooden posts, which are attached to house beams for further security.

The arrangement of the warp differs from the previously

26. A body-tension loom with a continuous warp from Lamalera on Lomblen. The weaver is turning the sword on its side in order to enlarge the counter-shed and thereby facilitate the smooth passage of the spool. (Copyright: Ruth Barnes.)

described loom because it is discontinuous: that is, it does not travel around the apparatus to complete a circle but is fastened to both the warp-beam and the breast-beam. As the fabric is woven it is rolled around the breast-beam and the unwoven warp is stored around the warp-beam, from where it can be let out as required.

These looms are usually equipped with a reed, which is a comb-like tool that helps to beat in the weft. The reed has teeth made from extremely hard slivers of bamboo gripped in a tight frame. The warp threads are slotted between the teeth and are thereby kept in place. During weaving the reed is used in conjunction with the sword to beat in the weft and in this technique the sword is gripped by the weaver with both hands and is knocked against the reed, which in turn pushes in the weft.

A hollow bamboo shuttle containing a spool usually carries the weft across the warp. The spool may be secured in the shuttle

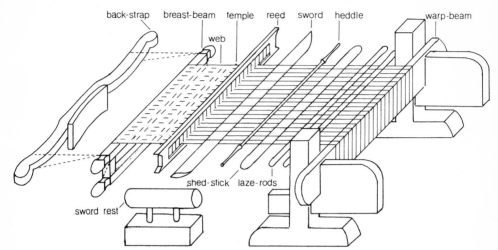

27. Diagram of a body-tension loom with a discontinuous warp.

case with a ball of cotton or by a weight fixed into the end of the
spool. Having a smooth surface, this shuttle can be knocked
swiftly through the sheds and is quicker than the type of spool
previously described.

Body-tension looms vary in size and shape, although the
principles of the two types described remain constant. A few
looms, however, are similar to the first type while including
features of the second kind. The width of cloth on all these looms
is governed by the width of the apparatus, which is limited by the
weaver's reach, and for wider garments several sections of cloth
have to be stitched together. The length of cloth woven with a
continuous warp is also restricted because it cannot be wound up

28. Examples of an Indonesian spool and shuttle.

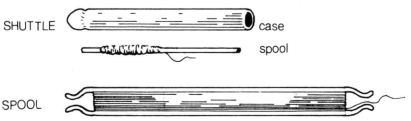

and therefore must be fully stretched during weaving, there being
a limit to the amount a weaver can keep in tension.

The shaft loom
    Various types of shaft loom are found in south-east Asia, and
in Indonesia they were used on the major islands as far east as
Bima and are still in operation in Java and north Bali. They differ
from the body-tension looms in the use of a frame to keep the
warp in tension instead of the weaver's body.
    As with the second kind of body-tension loom, the woven cloth
can be wound around a beam in front of the weaver, which is now

29. Diagram of a shaft loom.

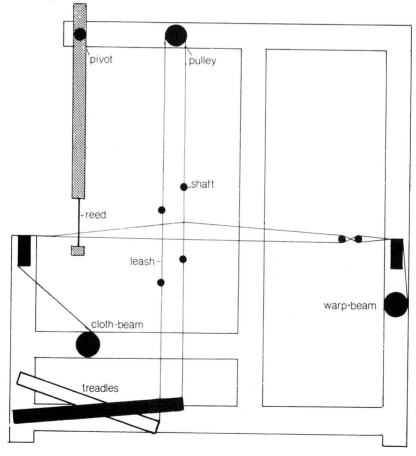

known as a cloth-beam. The warp-beam containing the unused thread can be either slotted into a support which is hung from the top of the loom's frame, or held between the two uprights at the back of the loom. A seat for the weaver in front of the breast-beam is sometimes built into the main frame.

The reed may have brass wire teeth and be considerably larger than those used on body-tension looms. It is hung from the top of the frame so that it can be swung to beat in the weft without recourse to a sword.

This loom is distinguished from the others by the different method of forming the sheds. In this case all the warp threads pass through leashes hung from two shafts (from which the loom receives its name) that are suspended above and across the warp. Further sets of leashes hang below the warp to join two more shafts suspended beneath the warp, each pair of upper and lower leashes thereby forming heddles that divide the shed and counter-shed. The heddles are connected by a pulley and bars hanging below the lower pairs of shafts serve as treadles to raise and lower them, one set raising the even threads and one the odd.

Modern variations of this loom may include heddles with eyes, as opposed to leashes, through which the warp passes. In Singaraja in Bali numerous shaft looms are fitted with European fly shuttles. The broadest cloth can be woven on these looms because the width is not restricted by the weaver's reach.

30. Measurements based on the body are used by Indonesian weavers.

Accessory equipment

In addition to the loom, the weaver may regularly use a wide variety of other items, many of which are produced locally. Needles of different shapes, sizes and materials are used everywhere, some of the most popular being carved from bone, horn and slivers of bamboo. These three versatile materials, and often cardboard, may also be used to make the small spools needed for the supplementary weft technique described in the next chapter. Other village-made tools include coconut fibre brushes bound with rattan strips, used to remove tangles from the warp, and small sharp knives forged from car suspension springs, useful for cutting thread.

If the weaver is using a body-tension loom, then she may sit on a comfortable palm-leaf mat surrounded by plaited baskets containing fresh yarn on spools in readiness for weaving and perhaps a betel-chewing kit. Should the weaver be disturbed or have to attend to other work she can quickly roll up her loom and tidy her gear away. The weaver at the shaft loom also works surrounded by her pieces of equipment, some placed on the bench beside her and others in baskets hung from the frame of the loom.

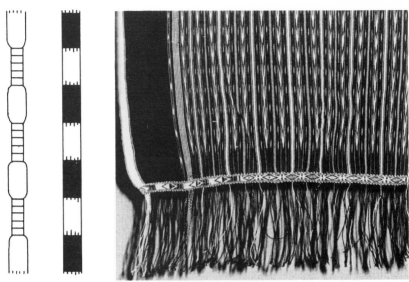

31. *(above left)* Diagram of a hank of cotton bound with an ikat resist and then shown after dyeing with the resist material removed.

32. *(above right)* The warp ikat technique is well suited to garments worn over the shoulder in pleats (Batak, Sumatra). Cotton in red, black and beige. 75½ by 26 inches (191 by 66 cm).

33. *(below)* A Buginese-style check woven by Biman craftswomen. Synthetic thread tabby weave in pink and black. 138 by 23½ inches (350 by 60 cm).

5
Decorative techniques

Ikat

The three related techniques known as ikat take their name from the Indonesian word *mengikat*, meaning 'to tie'. In all these techniques the designs are dyed on to at least some of the threads before they are woven, and, as is suggested by their collective name, this is brought about by tying something around the yarns that will resist the dye.

Warp ikat textiles from northern Sumatra, inner Kalimantan, Maluku and the province of East Nusa Tenggara are so named because it is the warp threads that are dyed before weaving. In these regions the dyer usually plans the distribution of the patterns by stretching out a continuous warp on a frame that simulates the loom. In this manner she works out approximately the extent of the design on the finished cloth and she is often aided by plans of successful patterns that have been recorded on lattices of bamboo and palm leaf or, more recently, on graph paper.

Dye-resistant palm leaves and sometimes rags are bound around selected bundles of warp threads, the finest textiles having ties around the smallest possible selection of yarns. When the area desired to remain undyed has been covered, the warp is dipped in a dye bath. The pattern is revealed by removing the resist material, but because the dye penetrates the edges of the material all the designs have the fuzzy outlines that characterise ikat. Different colours can be dyed on the same cloth by changing the position of the resist-protected areas. Craftswomen often commence dyeing with lighter colours so that extra shades can be obtained by overdyeing. Once the dyeing has been completed, the warp is carefully arranged on the loom to maintain the pattern.

Textiles of this kind are usually 'warp-faced': that is, the weft is beaten in so as to be virtually concealed, leaving the patterned warp in a more prominent and visible position. The use of the continuous warp allows the repetition of designs if the upper and lower planes are bound together with the same resist, and the 'mirror' images are popular on shoulder blankets. These garments are sometimes worn in pleats with the pattern flowing down either side of the body, an especially effective way of displaying the longitudinal haze of the warp ikat.

Weft ikat techniques are popular in north Bali and south Sumatra and, as their name indicates, are made by applying the resist dye method to the weft. Fabrics made in this manner may often be weft-faced, the weft being in a more prominent position. In the double ikat method, for which the Balinese of Tenganan are renowned, the resist material is applied to both warp and weft. It requires great skill to weave together patterns that have been dyed separately and the designs are usually married by pulling the threads into position with bone needles.

Bands, stripes and checks
Different-coloured stripes running the length of the warp are common in *sarungs* from central-east Lombok and Sumbawa and are often used as borders for ikat fabrics from Kalimantan, Timor, Roti, Flores and Sumba. The stripes are easily achieved by using a monochrome weft and a variously coloured warp in the

34. Examples of tapestry weaves.

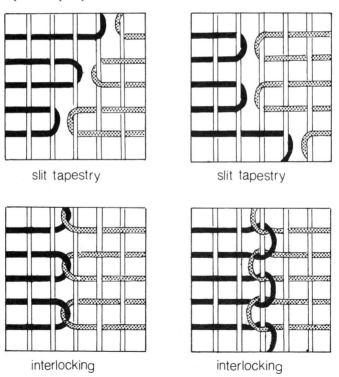

slit tapestry   slit tapestry

interlocking   interlocking

basic one-to-one weave known as tabby. Weft-banded fabrics can be made by using different-coloured wefts with a single-coloured warp, and checks are the result of combining stripes and bands. Checked *sarungs* are particularly popular with Indonesia's coastal Muslim traders, the Bugis and most ethnic groups in Sumbawa. Subtle differences in the arrangement of the checks often indicate the island of origin. Today, many cheap checked *sarungs* are manufactured in Javan factories and can be seen throughout the archipelago.

Tapestry

Although tapestry techniques are known in Sumatra and southern Sulawesi, it is on Sumbawa that they are most commonly used. These methods are employed when two wefts of different colours meet in the same plane, and because wefts used in this manner do not travel completely across the fabric they are said to be discontinuous. A slit is often formed between two discontinuous wefts and this may weaken the fabric if it is allowed to grow too long. The weakness can be prevented either by stepping the slits to form a diagonal pattern or by alternating them for a hatched effect. Adjacent areas of different hues can also be joined without slits by interlocking the opposing wefts; this method, however, leaves slightly raised wefts between each block of colour.

Tablet weaving

In tablet weaving coloured warps are fed through eyes in bone or wooden discs, which can be turned to raise different sheds. The coloured warp threads are thus twined into different positions, which are secured by shots of the weft. Patterns can be created by turning the tablets in a regular order, although resultant fabrics are usually narrow because of the limitations imposed by the size of the discs. Tablet weaving as practised by the Toraja has been described by Rita Bolland and it was once known to the Bimanese; this technique may, however, have been more widely distributed.

Float weaving

A weft shot is said to 'float' when it passes over two or more warps before being interwoven and thus differs from the tabby weave system of interlacing one warp to one weft. Attractive weaves can be made by alternating the amount of the floated weft on any one side. If the warp threads are a different colour from the weft then more of their hue will be visible on the non-floated side, giving the distinctive 'negative' effect used in Sumatra, Sumbawa, Sulawesi and Sumba.

Supplementary warp and weft

A supplementary weft is a decorative thread that is added to the basic weft of the ground weave and is therefore not structural. Supplementary threads are entered in the same sheds as the ordinary wefts but differ by being allowed to float over selected warps. Distinctive patterns can be formed when the supplementary threads are of a different colour or material from the ground weave.

These decorative threads may run continuously across the width of the fabric or across only part of it (i.e. discontinuous). Special pattern heddles may be introduced to raise selected warp threads and so govern the way in which the supplementary threads float. Complex designs can be woven with this technique, known as *songket,* by the use of serried ranks of pattern heddles that are raised and lowered in a regular order. The value of numerous heddles is illustrated in an old Biman ditty formerly sung by young women to their lovers in the army:

'Arrows in your shield can be used for heddles,
So go forward in battle, I'll hear no excuses.'

Alternatively, the supplementary threads can be introduced with a small spool or needle in a technique called *sungkit.* Here the weaver must keep to the pattern either by counting along the warp from memory or by using a diagram placed under the loom. The latter method allows for innovation during weaving, whereas with the former new ideas have to be incorporated at the planning stage, when the position of the heddles is ascertained. Some weavers may use both techniques, a complex repeat pattern being executed with the aid of heddles and minor flourishes being added with a small spool.

Supplementary weft techniques are widely used in Sumatra, Bali, Sulawesi, Lombok, coastal Kalimantan, Sumbawa and Sumba. In most of these islands, and particularly in Palembang and the Minankabau area of Sumatra, gold and silver supplementary threads may be used in conjunction with a silk ground weave. Less expensive textiles use cotton of synthetic supplementary wefts and it is becoming quite common to see these textiles with the name of the customer included in the weave. Supplementary weft is one of Indonesia's foremost and most versatile textile traditions.

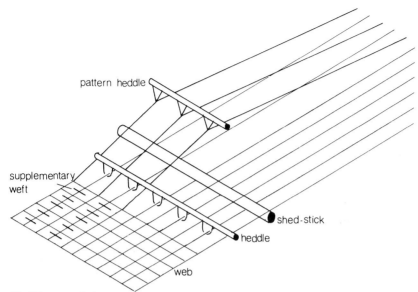

35. Diagram of the supplementary weft technique.

In the other form of supplementary weaving, additional pattern threads are laid in the warp. These threads are raised and lowered by pattern heddles so that they float on alternating sides of the warp along the length of the fabric. The technique is not as common as the supplementary weft variety, though it is well known in Sumba, Timor and Bali.

Batik

This is probably the most internationally famous of Indonesia's decorative techniques, yet it is not used throughout the archipelago. It is widely employed on the two most populous islands, Java and Madura. It is also found in Bali, west Lombok and central Sulawesi and used to be made in south Sumatra.

Batik is a resist method of dyeing woven cloth with the use of beeswax to repel the dye. Warm wax, which hardens as it cools, is applied to those parts of the design which will not receive the dye. After immersion in a dye bath the wax can be easily removed by gently washing the cloth in warm water. Numerous colours can be introduced by altering the resist areas on the cloth before it is dipped into a different dye. Generally the lighter hues are dyed

36. A Javan *canting* used for applying wax in the batik *tulis* process. (Copyright: Horniman Museum.)

37. A decorative clip used to secure textiles while the wax is applied with a *canting* in the batik *tulis* method. (Copyright: Horniman Museum.)

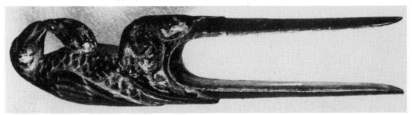

first to allow the possibility of overdyeing.

To speed production, wooden and brass stamps called *cap* were introduced in the nineteenth century. By this method patterns are produced in a mirror image on two blocks which are clamped on either side of the cloth. Repeat patterns of great complexity can be made, and today many of the stamps have themselves become collectors' items. Otherwise, the ancient hand-drawn *(tulis)* technique is used, warm wax being applied between carefully placed lines with an instrument called a *canting*. This tool consists of a brass tube leading from a reservoir that is supported by a wooden handle. The designer uses various sizes of *canting* to coat different areas. To ensure a smooth flow of wax, the reservoir is warmed over a candle flame before use. During the dyeing process some of the colour may run along fine cracks in the wax to form the spidery patterns that often characterise batik. Other substances, such as rice paste, may also serve as a batik resist, and these can be seen amongst the Sundanese of west Java.

The ancient courts of Java have produced some of the world's most elegant batiks, many of which were reserved exclusively for royal use. The industry is still very important in Java, with modern developments including bold and innovative high-fashion shirts.

Pelangi

The Indonesian word *pelangi* means 'rainbow', and this vividly describes the effect produced by a tie dye technique that is found principally in Java and Madura but is also known in Palembang and Bima. To achieve the patterns, sections of cloth are gathered together and bound tightly, the tied area and folds serving as a resist. After dyeing, the cloth can be untied to reveal the patterns. Sometimes bundles of cloth or pebbles are used to pad out and alter the dimensions of the dye receiving area. As with resist-dye techniques, the cloth can be retied and dyed for further embellishments. Designs produced in this manner have wavy or curved patterns that merge into each other at the edges, hence the rainbow title.

Tritik

This resist-dye method employs stitched thread rather than wax or bindings to control the spread of the colour. In this case the pattern is stitched over the cloth before it is dyed, the resist thread later being removed. The technique is principally associated with Java, though it is also used by Palembang dyers in conjunction with *pelangi* to produce exquisitely coloured shoulder cloths.

38. Diagram of a cloth tied with the *pelangi* method and then shown after dyeing with the resist removed.

Couching

This technique has the advantage of permitting the use of elements that are too stiff or heavy to be woven into the fabric. Thick metallic threads and ribbon, often in parallel rows, are sewn on to textiles in many parts of Indonesia, especially Nias, Sumatra, east Java, coastal Kalimantan and Sumbawa. Beads and feathers may be stitched on to textiles in inner Kalimantan, and pearls, semi-precious stones and small mirrors can be seen on garments from Bima, Ujung Pandang and the Lampung area of Sumatra.

Appliqué

Appliqué methods involve the addition to the main cloth of an accessory fabric, which is usually secured by sewing. In Java and Sumbawa an assortment of material may be sewn on to textiles, velvet especially being favoured. On Sumba the more attractive sections of old textiles are sewn on to new fabrics.

Painting and gilding

Bali adds to its great repertoire of textile techniques the use of painted cloth. Before the wide availability of industrially produced oils and acrylics, the Balinese obtained their pigments from many local sources: soot was used for black; white came from lime; red and brown from blood and iron-rich clays. The designs are usually sketched with a pencil and the painting is added with a brush or chewed twig.

Gold and silver leaf are applied with the aid of egg-white based glues to the surfaces of southern Balinese and central Javanese textiles. It has also been suggested that gilding is carried out with heat in Bali, although this method needs further investigation.

Embroidery

The use of decorative threads sewn on to a fabric is found on most textile-producing islands. In inner Kalimantan and East Nusa Tenggara embroidered borders can be seen on fabrics that are principally embellished with other decorative techniques. Occasionally, fine silver yarn may be added in a simple running stitch to cloth from Sumbawa and southern Sulawesi. One of the most common techniques, which involves long straight stitches running parallel to the weft, is known as pattern darning and this may often be difficult to distinguish from supplementary weft. Cross stitches, star eyelets and chain stitch are popular in north Sumatra.

Final notes

In a broad-ranging book such as this it has been possible to give some of the techniques only a brief explanation. Supplementary weft, for example, is a very varied and complex process and has been given only a brief introduction. Some techniques have received only partial coverage (gilding) or none at all (stencils) because so little has been written about them. In some cases field research is the only means of discovering practices that have long fallen into disuse, such as the Bimanese method of adding sheen to a fabric by ironing in the juice of special berries with a cowrie shell. For non-Indonesians there is much to be learned about the interpretation of designs and differences in aesthetics. Finally, it should be remembered that not only new techniques but new ways of utilising materials and of combining ideas are continually being incorporated into this rich and ever changing tradition.

39. Three techniques are combined in this woman's shoulder cloth from Palembang in Sumatra. Silk dyed in purple, orange, yellow and blue by *tritik* and *pelangi* methods; couched gilded threads. 85 by 30½ inches (216 by 78 cm). (Copyright: Museum of Mankind.)

40. A Hindu religious scene, painted in numerous colours, is depicted on this Balinese textile. Undyed cotton cloth woven in a tabby weave; red, black, green, yellow, ochre and blue pigments. 49½ by 13 inches (126 by 33 cm). (Copyright: Merseyside County Museums.)

6
Museums to visit

United Kingdom
Horniman Museum, London Road, Forest Hill, London SE23 3PQ. Telephone: 01-699 1872 or 2339 or 4911.
Merseyside County Museums, William Brown Street, Liverpool L3 8EN. Telephone: 051-207 0001 or 5451.
Museum of Mankind, (the Ethnography Department of the British Museum), 6 Burlington Gardens, London W1X 2EX. Telephone: 01-437 2224 or 2228.
Pitt Rivers Museum, South Parks Road, Oxford OX1 3PP. Telephone: Oxford (0865) 512541.
Royal Scottish Museum, Chambers Street, Edinburgh EHI 1JF. Telephone: 031-225 7534.

Australia
Australian Museum, 6-8 College Street, Sydney, New South Wales 2000.
Australian National Gallery, Canberra, ACT 2601.
University Museum, James Cook University, Townsville, Queensland 4811.

Canada
National Museum of Man, Victoria and Metcalfe Streets, Ottawa, Ontario K1A 0M8.

Germany
Museum of Ethnography, Schaumainkai 29, 6000 Frankfurt, Hessen.
Rautenstrauch-Joest-Museum, Ubierring 45, 5000 Köln (Cologne), Nordrhein-Westfalen.

Hungary
Museum of Ethnography, Könyves Kàlman Körút 40, Budapest VIII.

Indonesia
Municipal Museum, Palembang, Sumatra.
Provincial Museum, Mataram, Lombok, Nusa Tenggara Barat.
Textile Museum, Jakarta.

Netherlands
Ethnographical Museum, Agathaplein 4, 2611 HR, Delft, Zuid
Holland.
Museum of Geography and Ethnology, Willemskade 25, 3016
DM, Rotterdam, Zuid Holland.
Museum of the Tropics, Linnaeusstraat 2, 1092 AD Amsterdam,
Noord Holland.
National Museum of Ethnology, Steenstraat 1, 2300 AE Leiden,
Zuid Holland.

Poland
Asia and Pacific Museum, ul Nalczowska 40, Warsaw.

United States of America
American Museum of Natural History, 79th Street and Central
Park West, New York, NY 10024.
Peabody Museum of Archaeology and Ethnology, 11 Divinity
Avenue, Cambridge, Massachusetts 02138.
Smithsonian Institution, 1000 Jefferson Drive, SW, Washington
DC 20560.
Textile Museum, 2320 South NW, Washington DC 20008.
University Museum, University of Pennsylvania, 33rd and Spruce
Streets, Philadelphia, Pennsylvania 19104.

7
Further reading

Clabburn, P. *The Needleworker's Dictionary.* Macmillan, 1976.
Gittinger, Mattiebelle. *Splendid Symbols: Textiles and Tradition
in Indonesia.* Washington Textile Museum, 1979.
Haddon, A. C., and Start, L. E. *Iban or Sea Dyak Fabrics and
their Patterns.* Ruth Bean, 1982 (first published 1933).
Hall, D. G. C. *A History of South-East Asia.* Macmillan, 1976.
Langewis, L., and Wagner, F. A. *Decorative Art in Indonesian
Textiles.* Mouton, 1964.
Larsen, Jack, L. *The Dyer's Art: Ikat, Batik, Plangi.* Van
Nostrand Reinhold, 1976.
Solyom, Bronwen, and Solyom, Garrett. *Textiles of the Indo-
nesian Archipelago.* Hawaii University Press, 1973.
Wagner, A. R. *Indonesia: The Art of an Island Group.* Methuen,
1959.

Index

Page numbers in italics refer to illustrations. References to islands in this index include references to towns and ethnic groups on those islands.

Ancient designs 5, *7,* 18, *19*
Appliqué 51
Bajo Laut 12
Bali 6, 12, 23, 24, 26, 33, 38, 41, 46, 48, 49, 52, *53*
Barnes, R. 39
Barnes, R. H. 32
Batik 5, 6, *11, 13, 16,* 49, 50
Bolland, R. 47
Bühler, A. 33, 34
Buton 21
Cedroth, S. 21
Checks *25,* 44, 47
Cotton *7, 11, 13, 16,* 20, 22, 23, 24, 25, 27-30, *34, 53*
Couching 51, *53*
Custom-made 5, 15, 18, 48
Design aids 18
Destar 25, 26
Domestic production 15, 16
Dyes 5, 11, 24, 30-35
Economic significance 5, 15, 17, 19, 21, 27, 32
Embroidery 51
Factory production 15, *25,* 47
Float weaves *31,* 47, 48
Flores 25, 46
Foreign influences 5, *7,* 10, *11,* 18, 32, 33
Gilding *13,* 51
Gin 27, 28
Gittinger, M. 21
Heddle 2, 36, 48
Ikat 6, *7,* 18, *19, 23,* 24, *44,* 45, 46
Irian Jaya 6, 12
Ironing 52
Java 5, 6, 10, 12, 13, 15, *16,* 18, 21, 24, 26, 27, 28, 32, 33, 41, 47, 49, 50, 51, 52
Kain 16, 24, 26
Kalimantan 5, 6, 12, 26, 34, 35, 38, 45, 46, 48, 51
Lomblen 22, *39*

Lombok 21, 46, 48, 49
Looms 2, *14,* 17, 36-43
Madura 12, 26, 49, 51
Maluku 10, 45
Metallic threads 19, 30, 31, 51, 52
Nias 19, 51
Nusa Tenggara 6, 10, 18, 26, 38, 45, 52
Painting 51, *53*
Pelangi 51, *53*
Riau 35
Roti 26, 33, 46
Sarung 24, 25, 26, 47
Sawu 26
Schools 17
Selendang 14, 25, 26, 31, *53*
Selimut 24, 25, 26
Shuttle and spool 2, 37, 39, 40
Silk *19,* 30
Sizing 37
Social significance 5, *13,* 15, 17-24
Spindle and spinning wheel 28-30
Sulawesi 10, 12, 17, 18, 19, 26, 27, 28, 33, 35, 38, 47, 48, 49, 51, 52
Sumatra 5, 10, 12, 19, 21, *22,* 23, *32,* 34, 45, 46, 47, 48, 49, 51, 52
Sumba *7,* 18, 19, *20,* 46, 48, 51
Sumbawa 6, *14,* 17, 20, 21, 24, 25, 28, 29, 31, 33, 34, 35, 38, 41, 46, 48, 51, 52
Supplementary weft and warp 2, *7, 20, 22, 34,* 48, 49
Swift 30, *31*
Sword 2, 39
Synthetic thread 30, *31*
Tabby weave *44,* 47
Tablet weaving 47
Tanimbar 35
Tapestry weaves *31, 46,* 47
Timor 10, 12, 19, 23, 26, 27, 34, 35, 46, 48
Tourism 5, 15, *16*
Tritik 51, *53*